Carousel

Essays and Such

Jeanne Powell

REGENT PRESS
Berkeley, California

Paperback
ISBN 13: 978-1-58790-266-6
ISBN 10: 1-58790-266-4
Library of Congress Control Number: 2014930981

E-book
ISBN 13: 978-1-58790-267-3
ISBN 10: 1-58790-267-2

Cover Photo by Jeanne Powell

Cover Design by Mark Weiman

Manufactured in the U.S.A.
REGENT PRESS
Berkeley, California
www.regentpress.net

ACKNOWLEDGEMENTS

[3] and *[4]* of *City Scenes* first appeared in
POETS ELEVEN 2012
anthology published by San Francisco Public Library, 2012

My Worst Vacation...Ever
was published on gadling.com for AOL Media in 2010

Versions of other essays appeared at *sidewalkstv.com*

Contents

2008 Election – Why Hillary Lost (2009) / 9

Rev. Jackson's Tears (2009) / 13

Helping Us See What Was (2011) / 18

Lincoln (2012) / 21

The Conspirator (2011) / 24

My Worst Vacation…Ever (2010) / 28

Fabulation, or the Re-education of Undine (2011) / 35

Fela! (2011) / 37

12 Years A Slave (2013) / 39

My Big Adventure (2009) / 44

The Business of Bowing (2009) / 48

The Invisible War (2012) / 50

Connections (2013) / 56

Elysium (2013) / 59

Vantage Point (2008) / 63

The Other Boleyn Girl (2009) / 65

Mad Money (2008) / 68

The Iron Lady (2012) / 70

Those Women In Veils (2009) / 74

When A Legend Visits (2012) / 79

The Company You Keep (2013) / 82

City Scenes (2010) / 86

2008 Election
Why Hillary Lost

A WINNER HAS BEEN DECLARED in the 2008 presidential election, thus averting another Constitutional crisis (as in 1876 and in 2000). Remarkably few ballot boxes were found floating in rivers this time around. Chads clinging to paper ballots were nowhere in sight.

Barack Hussein Obama is an exotic choice. Raised partly in Indonesia with an Asian stepfather and partly in the state of Hawaii by an American grandmother, Barack Hussein was born to a Muslim father from Kenya. He was a toddler during the brutal era of political assassinations. He is not the descendant of slaves. And he could very well be the first Black president. Given the racial history of the United States, we may never know for sure about his presidential predecessors.

Hillary Rodham Clinton was the most qualified of all the candidates who endured the political primary season. When you read Gail Sheehy's riveting biography, *Hillary's Choice*, you discover her brilliant background and realize that contemporaries spoke of her as a future U.S. president when she was still an undergraduate. If only Hillary

Rodham had taken the road less traveled, instead of a 30 year detour to Arkansas to marry the Rhodes scholar with whom she fell in love!

Six factors seemed to influence the choice of Barack as the DEM party candidate:

[1] the fear of women;

[2] party bosses keeping quiet about Senator John Edwards' adultery during primary season;

[3] Senator Ted Kennedy's irritation with former President Bill Clinton for his remarks critical of Obama;

[4] fact that Oprah Winfrey accompanied Barack to Iowa presidential caucuses;

[5] Barack's relative "nonblackness" compared to Shirley Chisholm, Al Sharpton, Jesse Jackson, Martin Luther King – we have Joe Biden's early slip of the tongue here;

[6] America's settler guilt about the African holocaust, Middle Passage, and slave labor camps (plantations) before the British navy brought an end to the international slave trade.

Chief among these is the fear of women in high office. About two dozen nations around the world have elected female leaders – presidents, prime ministers, chancellors, premiers – in the last three generations. The United States is not among them.

A published study of media coverage during the 2008 presidental primary campaign revealed a clear bias against Senator Hillary Rodham Clinton. Articles referring to her cleavage, hair style, ankles, alleged emotional state or previous marital trouble too often were substituted for reporting on her political views and accomplishments.

This bias was nonpartisan and extended to coverage

of Governor Sarah Palin when she was VP candidate on the GOP ticket. Media hostility included questioning the *maternity* of Sarah's infant son, criticizing her teenage daughter, commenting on her campaign wardrobe and slamming her blue collar origins.

I wrote a three-page poem, "About That Woman," which can be found in WORD DANCING; concentrated on voter registration issues; read Robin Morgan's powerful essay on why she supported Hillary for president; fumed about the pressure placed on Dr. Maya Angelou to withdraw her support of Hillary; and listened to Bill Moyers on his PBS Journal talk about the sad state of the process in general. And I voted for former Congresswoman Cynthia McKinney on a third-party ticket.

And I distanced myself from "all that," or thought I had. I truly thought I had. One evening after the national vote, I was watching BBC World cover Barack's triumphant return to Chicago. He was about to speak, outside on a stage, with enthusiastic crowds. Something was different about the scene and it took me a moment to see it, to take it all in. Two clear glass walls, one on either side of the stage, that's all. Suddenly I could not breathe and had to sit down.

Then I recalled why I would not allow myself to be drawn in by this laconic newcomer who was born too late to remember. I had sat with my parents, experiencing five funerals in six years, through the immediacy of television. Those leaders left too soon, creating a vacuum no one could fill.

So much adulation, underlined with desperation, heaped upon this stranger. So many people need a hero now, it seems, preferably a male, yes, it still needs to be a male. They all want me to believe, because they don't know what I know, or just don't want to remember what I can't forget.

In the time before glass walls
mourners dressed in long black veils
a grieving nation stunned by losses
caissons pulled by beasts of burden
empty boots reversed in stirrups
muffled drums and flags at half mast
midnight vigils over coffins
Myrlie Evers, Betty Shabazz
Coretta Scott King
Jacqueline and Ethel Kennedy,
in the time before glass walls.

So in 2008 I voted on every local issue; exhorted others to the polls; handed my book, WORD DANCING, to Hillary Clinton that summer at a fundraiser in Silicon Valley; and renewed my passport (just in case the election went the other way). On inauguration day 2009, I walked along the Embarcadero and watched seagulls in flight.

JEANNE POWELL

Rev. Jackson's Tears

SO MUCH TO CELEBRATE last November 5th, the day after America's 2008 national election. The Chicago audience was giddy with excitement as the incoming president spoke. No reason to notice an older man standing quietly in the crowd, tears running down his face, features twisted with emotion. Once the photograph was published, though, responses were quick – twitters, smug columns and lightweight editorials, cartoons and yawns.

During Obama's speech, many people across the country waited for some recognition of the pioneers and martyrs whose sacrifices paved the way. And that recognition came in a few graceful phrases, too few, before the photogenic president-elect moved on. Of course, he was president of all the country, and his speech must reflect that reality.

Jesse Jackson Sr. has grown old in service to the civil rights movement. He walked and sat in and demonstrated with Dr. King and the other ministers of the SCLC, and continued serving after Dr. King was assassinated. So many events Jackson witnessed and experienced after answering the call in 1960, leaving school to work in the

Movement. He did not have an Ivy League education or middle class upbringing. Like so many civil rights pioneers, he brought what he had, brought all he had, and went where he had to go.

Rev. Jackson was blessed to have walked with greatness, and to have inspired thousands of African American youth who otherwise would have fallen through the cracks in our fractured, race-oriented society. In 1971 he formed PUSH, People United to Serve Humanity, and campaigned for economic empowerment of the disadvantaged and people of color. In 1984 he formed National Rainbow Coalition to concentrate on issues of social justice and political empowerment. And he ran for president in 1984 and 1988.

Go back to those incredible years in the library and Internet videos, and look at the faces of America's majority newscasters, as they exhibit irritation, impatience and actual fear that Rev. Jackson was taking precious votes away from Democrat frontrunners in presidential primaries. The historic nature of his effort, following in the footsteps of Frederick Douglass and Shirley Chisholm, was lost on them.

After nearly 200 years, there came a time when Christian ministers no longer led the way in African American culture – after hundreds of slave uprisings; the Civil War; the lynching and burning alive of African Americans by domestic terrorists; violent assaults on African American communities in the 1920s; all the marches and sit-ins by those who practiced passive resistance, plagued by death threats and assassination attempts in the 1960s. Other civil rights advocates were spat upon or shot or beaten to death for asking for the right to eat at a cafe, ride on a Greyhound bus, register to vote, send children of color to integrated schools.

It came to pass that their time was then, was then, not now. Business professionals and attorneys from the African American community, men and women successful in the secular world, moved forward and ran for public office on every level, to cement the changes, illustrate the progress made by those ministers, nuns, priests, rabbis, students, farm workers, homemakers, and revolutionaries like Stokely Carmichael of SNCC so long ago.

Ghosts were present that day in November 2008, and Jesse Jackson clearly felt their weight. Civil rights volunteers kidnapped and murdered in secret, others shotgunned as they drove cars to help local activists, and others clubbed to death on public streets in the south. Schwerner, Chaney, Goodman. Viola Liuzzo, whose murder left a husband and two young sons in Michigan, the state where I spent most of my childhood. Four little girls in a Birmingham AL church.

The many threats against Dr. King when he took the Movement north for housing integration marches in Illinois and when he led strong opposition to the American war in Vietnam. Medgar Evers, NAACP leader, shot from ambush as he pulled into his driveway one night. President Kennedy brought Evers' widow to the White House, and Evers was buried in Arlington National Cemetery. That same year JFK was murdered in Texas. Charles Evers and Robert Kennedy formed a close friendship; both had lost brothers in public service.

"At the bottom of the Atlantic Ocean there is a railroad made of human bones, black ivory, black ivory..." Amiri Baraka reminds us. The most notorious holocaust in human history occurred from the mid-1500s to mid-1800s; European historians estimate that as many as 100,000,000 human beings were kidnapped from west, central and east Africa. Half of those kidnapped died during the brutal voyage of the Middle Passage and their corpses were thrown overboard. Slave labor camps of the Second World War took their inspiration from slave labor practices on plantations in North America, South America and the Caribbean, before the abolition of the international slave trade in the middle of the 19th century.

A titanic struggle to end slavery and preserve the Union took place between 1861 and 1865, but it did not end there. Douglas A. Blackmon in his book, *Slavery By Another Name*, has written of the systematic re-enslavement of Blacks after the Civil War, even before the end of Reconstruction, and continuing until World War II. Well researched and horrific to read. How strange that we continue to condemn European countries for their wartime evil, without exploring also the deep horrors of racial brutality in this country.

So many gone...so much suffering...so much violence aimed at an entire people in order to justify using their slave labor to build the wealthiest economy in the history of the world. Racism remains the bloodstained elephant with broken tusks in the center of the room, as people tiptoe around it, eyes averted, looking for an easy way out.

Yes, there were tears on Rev. Jackson's face the day Obama spoke about his presidential victory. Yes, there were many around the country who would have liked Obama to visit the segregated graves of the Black Civil War veterans in Arlington National Cemetery, and the civil rights memorial designed by Maya Lin in the south, and the bones taken from slave graveyards discovered during excavation for new construction projects.

Time remains, and abides. After all, the ghosts of our ancestors remain with us always. And Jesse Jackson's tears spoke of many rivers to cross, of dreams deferred, and the absence of a crystal staircase for generations of African Americans.

Helping Us See What Was

LAST SUNDAY AFTERNOON I was shopping at Whole Foods, taking advantage of its reasonably priced "house label" to get maximum value, and I overheard two women talking about reactions among friends who had seen "The Help." We related instantly, perhaps because of the high visibility of the film, and perhaps because of the energy shared by those who have "been in the storm."

I volunteered that I had written a review of the film. They wanted to talk, so we decided to meet for brunch and continue the dialogue, and I do mean "dialogue." They felt no need to slam the film on all fronts from a polished ebony platform, which was refreshing.

Writing a review of "The Help" was difficult. I thought it was important not to judge the director and the writer by standards unrealistic for them. This is a commercial film adapted from a book recording one woman's experience after she returned to the Deep South with a new perspective.

I have talked with a lot of people, from poets laureate to people's grandparents, and one thing that stands out is a gulf between what blue-collar people of color experienced and what some members of the Talented Tenth want to see portrayed.

We did not all look like Halle Berry. Bodies grew thick from hard work, and from food which was more filling than nutritious. We did not all speak like Toni Morrison; many of us never saw the inside of a secondary school or had time to read any book except the Christian Bible, and we read that book to give us the strength to keep on keeping on. Fried chicken was on everyone's menu, period. And we could not speak our minds back then without serious, even life-threatening, consequences. It may help to re-read the lyrics to a song recorded by Billie Holliday decades ago, "Strange Fruit."

There are privileged African American youth in this country today who have no idea what "the help" endured back then. This film may help them. There are millions of majority Americans who believe slavery was like the film "Gone With The Wind," that it ended with the Civil War, and who have not read the book *Slavery By Another Name* (from the end of Reconstruction until World War II). This film may help them as well.

It is important to trust the instincts of the two actresses who portray domestic servants in this film. And it is important to realize that interactions between women will always remain outside center stage as long as men write the official histories. After all, the white civic leaders who chose to wait out the Montgomery AL bus boycott of 1955-1956 had no idea their wives would object to losing their domestic help; they never thought to ask the women anything. So, the changing relationship between

Sissy Spacek and Whoopi Goldberg in "The Long Walk Home" is a significant but little-noticed part of the civil rights experience, as is the connection between the budding journalist in "The Help" and the domestic servants of color in her home town. Her changed perspective, after attending college in the North and returning to the South, opens a door on a way of life which had a profound impact on African American families in the southeast from 1876 through the 1960s.

Our national inability or unwillingness to place slavery, the Civil War and continued racial discrimination in historical perspective presents daily challenges for so many. "Living While Black" still remains a life-threatening experience in many parts of the United States.

Something film critic Mick LaSalle wrote in his Sunday column in the *San Francisco Chronicle* a while ago caught my attention. Perhaps our collective unconsciousness about the war which tore this country apart – the Civil War (1861-1865) – needs to be addressed?

"...And so our national culture has turned itself inside out ignoring that the Confederacy was a disgrace – that the leaders who brought it about were uncomfortably close to Nazis, willing to ruin the Earth's last best hope for the sake of perpetuating an absolutely evil institution [slavery], which they not only wanted to maintain but also to extend all the way to the Pacific and into Central and South America.... and they came closer to obliterating this great country than Adolf Hitler ever did in his wildest dreams...."

JEANNE POWELL

Lincoln

DIRECTOR STEPHEN SPIELBERG's Oscar-worthy film is adapted from historian Doris Kearns Goodwin's 2005 best-seller, *Team of Rivals: The Political Genius of Abraham Lincoln*. Tony Kushner's screenplay is ambitious and successful with a difficult subject including a furious mix of ambivalent politicians.

It is January 1865 and starving rebel soldiers begin to desert the southern insurrection. General William Tecumseh Sherman is preparing to march his federal troops through North and South Carolina. President Abraham Lincoln is doing battle with powerful political enemies and competitors in his cabinet and on Capitol Hill. Keep your friends close, it has been said, and keep your enemies closer. Lincoln knew the wisdom of these words as he presided over a young nation which had to be reunited at all costs.

Those men and women of the American Civil War are larger than life today because they grappled with historic issues during a turbulent era; their actions, reactions and decisions held serious consequences for all who came after them. The veteran cast of "Lincoln" gives us those moments in captivating scenes and compelling performances.

Daniel Day-Lewis creates a Lincoln we can believe – torn and at times tormented but determined to face the issue of slavery as it affected the nation. It is the nation that concerns President Lincoln, whether a country can survive half slave and half free, and if not then what must be done to bring the country together again.

Sally Field would not be everyone's first choice to play Mary Todd Lincoln, but she wins over the skeptics with her fiery energy and almost maniacal devotion to her troubled husband and to her sons, both the living and the dead. At a White House reception, her barbed banter with her husband's political opponents in Congress is highly amusing.

Tommy Lee Jones plays the eloquent radical Republican who led the "bloody-shirt" Reconstructionists after the murder of President Lincoln; he is marvelous as Thaddeus Stevens. Stevens' views on the abolition of slavery are far to the left of Lincoln and the nation holds its breath to see if those two strong-willed men can compromise. Intrigue, secret meetings, not so gentle conspiracies, and at times hilarious scheming are the order of the day.

Abraham Lincoln loved humorous moments and could tell a good tale with subtlety and wit. The film gives us many such moments from Daniel Day-Lewis. James Spader's antics as a lower-echelon pol charged with buying votes to guarantee passage of the thirteenth amendment provide another brand of humor. Politics has not changed much since then.

There are brief but notable performances from S. Epatha Merkerson as Lydia Smith, the Black widow who is Thaddeus Stevens' secret wife, and Gloria Reuben as Elizabeth Keckley, personal assistant to Mary Todd Lincoln.

"Lincoln" resonates on multiple levels – wrenching battle scenes of hand-to-hand combat; the president visiting troops in the field during a rainstorm; a first lady still mourning the loss of her middle son; Mary Todd Lincoln raging at her husband to prevent him from allowing their oldest son to enlist in the army; Thaddeus Stevens' dilemma over whether to support the thirteenth amendment which is weaker than it should be.

Does the U.S. need this amendment at all? Congress has declared war, and the president has special war powers. The Union is winning the war on the battlefield. But will there be a legal dilemma once the war ends and the president no longer has extraordinary war powers? Can't we just send "them" back to the African continent? How can "we" live with them once they are free?

I need this amendment to cure slavery and this pestilential war, the president says. And in the face of southern intransigence: Lose the freedom to oppress, and you may gain other freedoms.

A thought-provoking film, "Lincoln" is historic in its presentation of the complex issues which still haunt a nation whose national economy was built on slavery, and entertaining as we witness the struggles unfold amid personal agendas, power plays, human foibles and deeply held hope.

The Conspirator

ROBERT REDFORD HAS PRODUCED a spectacular historical film, sure to garner multiple Academy Award nominations.

The conspirator in the film title is a noncombatant and a woman, the first woman to be executed by the federal government. More than 500 women and girls were hanged for crimes in various North American colonies, territories and states between 1632 and 1937. Mrs. Surratt was the first to be convicted by a military tribunal.

Mary Surratt is a widow and mother who runs a boardinghouse and owns other real estate in the Washington, D.C. area. Several of her boarders turn out to be the men who kill President Abraham Lincoln, plan to murder Vice President Andrew Johnson, and seriously wound Secretary of State William Seward in April 1865.

That there was a conspiracy to cripple the U.S. government in 1865 is not in doubt. Whether Mary Surratt was involved, or just protecting her adult son, is unclear even today. What is clear, however, is that the United States was still a new nation, less than a century old, and had been torn apart by a bloody Civil War. While General

Ulysses Grant receives Robert Lee's surrender on behalf of the southern rebels, 20 rebel armies still remain in the field. When President Lincoln is assassinated, the capitol city and the nation are thrown into a frenzy of fear. Radical Republicans in Congress wave the "bloody shirt" and seek revenge on the southern states which committed treason by seceding from the Union. Secretary of War Edwin Stanton wants the murderous conspirators caught, tried, convicted and hanged – not necessarily in that order.

In this setting of fear and chaos, director Robert Redford introduces us to the main characters. James McAvoy is convincing as the battle-scarred veteran (Frederick Aiken) who simply wants to practice law and marry his sweetheart. Suddenly he is asked to be second chair in the defense of Mary Surratt. Aiken has seen his comrades die in a brutal war. Wounded twice in battle, he experiences the shock of his president and commander-in-chief being cut down by assassins. He believes Surratt to be guilty and does not wish to defend her.

Robin Wright gives a fine performance as the widow Mary Surratt, who describes herself as "a southerner, a Catholic and a devoted mother." It is as a mother that Surratt fights against her attorney, even at the risk of her own life. Wright portrays her as strong and independent, having survived marriage to a drunkard and raised children. How Surratt and her attorney Aiken slowly establish communication and trust is at the heart of this powerful film.

The other conflict swirls around the Secretary of War, well played by Kevin Kline. America is at war, in the most devastating kind of hostility, a nation divided against itself. Secretary of War Stanton does not want to leave anything to chance. Enemies of the state must be hunted down and punished. The Constitution itself must be suspended, in order to save it, or so it seems. Should a civilian be tried by a military court? It is more than a year after Surratt's execution before the Supreme Court issues a decision on that question.

How Frederick Aiken defends Mary Surratt under these impossible conditions, and why Secretary of War Edwin Stanton feels the nation must be protected from further chaos at all costs, set the stage.

Redford skillfully directs from a script by James Solomon. Solomon began writing "The Conspirator" in 1993; he came to screenwriting after a career as a journalist. His script is well researched, beginning with his reading actual transcripts of Surratt's trial. The producers hired historians to double check the facts and to help set the visuals.

Special credit goes to production designer Kalina Ivanov, costume designer Louise Frogley and director of photography Newton Thomas Sigel for their ensemble work. It turns out that the city of Savannah GA is a good match for 1865 Washington. General Sherman was able to spare that city during his march to the sea, so it retains much of the original architecture of the period. Says Kalina Ivanov, "Everything in our film is gaslight or kerosene or candlelight. Everything is organic to the period."

A brief turn by Evan Rachel Wood as Anna Surratt, daughter of the conspirator, holds your attention. Anna is placed under house arrest during her mother's trial. She is called upon to make a hard choice, one which places Anna in conflict with her mother, and Wood recreates that torment vividly.

The shock of the well-planned conspiracy. The drama of hunting and capturing the assassins. The intensity of the courtroom scenes. Civil War veteran Frederick Aiken asks: "Why did I fight for the Union if my rights are not assured?" Secretary of War Edwin Stanton says: "To ensure the survival of this nation, I would do anything." Regardless of your perspective, you will come away from this film with appreciation for the subject matter and how well it is handled.

My Worst Vacation ... Ever

COME TO MY LOVELY HOME in the Sierra foothills and be transformed in four days of pampering and meditation, Emelda whispered, weaving through guests at a crowded art reception. She distributed homemade brochures and cookies laced with a delicious ... herb. What a sweet person, I thought, as she moved among us in a long flowing skirt with contrasting silk blouse and large gold earrings. What deep dark magical eyes, and she had such a radiant smile. Her brightly colored brochure spoke of yoga stretches at sunrise, deep meditation at midday, delicious homecooked meals, stunning views of nature, and a gentle atmosphere of healing and laughter. Just what I needed after a hellish three months of working for a grubby nonprofit in the East Bay where political infighting had been taken to a whole new low. Beauty, inner joy, peace were promised by this brochure and her reassuring smile.

Of course, I couldn't wait to find out more about Emelda's wonderful retreat. The Sierra foothills were lower levels of the Sierra Nevada Mountains, she said, including towns on the border between California and

Nevada. One could take the train or she could arrange a carpool. Payment was by check or credit card. About six like-minded men and women would attend. She had been doing retreats for years, she said, and was an experienced group leader, along with her husband. Bring hiking boots and warm sweaters since it will be January in the foothills.

As Emelda continued to circulate and charm during the art reception, I chatted with her husband. Lawrence said his wife was trained as what most people might call a witch, but she was more than that. She had been initiated as a shaman by some guy in Mexico, and she was a wonderful healer. Now we all know there are good witches and bad witches – we've seen the musical "Wicked" – but Lawrence's reassuring smile told me there was nothing to fear. And in college I had read a Carlos Castenada book about shamans – healers trained in Latin American traditions – so the whole thing did not seem too scary. To raise money for this little vacation, I held a "garage sale" in the courtyard of my apartment building, divesting myself of paperback books, copper colanders, rhinestone bracelets, two-inch sandals – anything I hadn't used in six months. After emptying the flower pot of silver dollars in my kitchen – a gift from an admirer – I deposited everything in the credit union and wrote a check to Emelda and Lawrence.

How little I knew about what lurked in the picturesque foothills of the Sierra Nevada Mountains. Because the hostess of this retreat to hell was a bona fide witch, and may have put us under all sorts of spells, I cannot even now be certain where this took place, not unless I go into deep trance to return to that state of mind, and I'm not willing to go there again, ever. The nearest town was miles away and downhill. Was it Auburn? Chinese Camp? Fiddletown? Placerville? Were we on the California side or the Nevada side? Will we ever know?

What I do remember is that I took the train along the California coast to my destination, and was met at the depot by others who had driven. Those of us without vehicles piled into two Land Rovers driven by Emelda and Lawrence. We drove uphill until the four-wheel drive failed. All vehicles then parked by the roadside and we trekked uphill for a mile, dragging our luggage in the warm mud. Their little abode was smaller than I anticipated, and it was clear there was no mail or pizza delivery to this desolate place. Icy sleet was falling. An unsightly propane tank filled the small yard; apparently it provided heat for the wooden house. By this time everyone was hungry. Emelda said it was too late to cook, so we ate cold porridge. I have hated porridge, hot or cold, since my childhood. However, one fierce look from her was all it took to silence me.

A neighbor was waiting to surrender Emelda's toddler son; no one had told us about the child. To spare the generator, we were shown to our sleeping area by candlelight. This was not starting out well – not at all.

Those who registered early and paid full price for the retreat received private rooms. Since I had paid sliding scale at the last minute, I slept on a floor mattress with quilts. The thermostat was turned down considerably at night so Lawrence and Emelda could save fuel. I shivered under the quilts, which smelled of dog. Turned out there was a large dog in the house, in addition to a small child. The dog barked, the child cried, and my neighbor on the other floor mattress snored. Well, so much for sleeping that first night!

We did not get up for yoga stretches at sunrise as promised, because Emelda and Lawrence were having really noisy sex in the bedroom down the hall and they took a nap afterward. Slowly the rest of us found the two bathrooms and then walked into the kitchen to search out food. The cupboard was bare. We munched on stale peanuts and ripe bananas. The happy hosting couple, nicely satiated, tumbled into the kitchen after a while and announced that food was being delivered in a bit; they simply had not had time to shop before retrieving us the previous day. And Emelda had to take time to nurse Baby Jeremy before they met us at the train station. Nursing? The kid was three years old! Nonetheless, she nursed.

The two of them squabbled with abandon about the day's schedule. Lawrence stamped out to walk the dog and Emelda nursed Baby Jeremy. The rest of us scratched our heads and looked at each other. At least the view from picture windows in two walls of the living room was breathtaking, and snow was falling everywhere. I had not seen such snow since I left the Great Lakes. This moment proved to be a fitting metaphor for the entire four days – guests left to their own devices while the happy couple played house, contrasted with the beauty of snow falling all day long on towering evergreens, three days out of four.

Later Emelda fussed with her two ancestor altars in the family room while Lawrence brought in wood and started a fire in the fireplace. Turned out we paying guests were supposed to cook for ourselves and then wash dishes afterward. Emelda directed us in a harsh smoky voice, not at all like the dulcet tones she used at the art reception. Her hair was flying everywhere and she padded about barefoot in a midnight-blue granny gown with unleashed breasts swinging from side to side, Baby Jeremy resting on one hip. The huge Doberman jumped up and licked each of us now and then, without warning. Oh, it was grand!

Yoga stretches? Well, not exactly. Emelda read them from a book, barely giving us time to get into position, let alone stretch. And there was almost room to stretch, once we pushed eight pair of muddy hiking boots out of the way. Meditation each day was interrupted by the need to change Baby Jeremy's diapers and nurse him, and by Emelda's persistent cough. Would you believe she smoked cigarillos? Like a chimney! While the hosts were busy with domestic chores, we poor dupes were supposed to write affirmations. "What's an affirmation?" one guest inquired. Emelda ignored him.

Food did reach us in this desolate place, finally: Raw potatoes, onions, cabbage, rutabagas, rice, pasta, salami, beer, Rocky Road ice cream. Lots of seasonings in the kitchen along with a large can of Crisco for cooking. Crisco – as in solid at room temperature?! OK, then. We guests made the best of it. What else could we do?

Everyone stayed inside because our hostess had a tropical personality and was not inclined toward the outdoors. In contrast, her husband was dressed in the latest Land's End outdoor gear and seemed to enjoy the weather. After three days of claustrophobia, I broke out and ran into the snow. Three feet of good packing snow, reminiscent of a Canadian winter without the freezing temperatures.

Throwing myself on my back, I laughed hysterically and moved my arms up and down to make snow angels. Lawrence came outside and joined me, while everyone else peered through the windows, looking puzzled by our antics. We threw snowballs at each other. When I started to build a snowman, Emelda's outdoorsy husband went inside to get a hat and scarf for my wintry creation. I knelt in the snow, looking for small rocks to complete the snowman's face.

Lawrence returned with suitable gear for my snowman. He took me on a tour of evergreen trees nearby, pausing on the far side of a particularly lush tree looming overhead.

"I like your energy," he said with an inviting smile. "You looked 16 while you were lying in the snow, like you really were enjoying yourself. You know, I grew up in snow country, chopping wood, handling horses. And I love it up here. We could make love right under this tree – no problem – and no one could even see us, just a hawk overhead or a fox running across the snow. My wife and I have an open relationship. Nothing is off limits..." He was standing so close I could smell the spearmint on his breath.

Open marriage? Virility in the snow? Foxes running under my feet? Burned cabbage percolating in my intestine? Good grief! I marveled at his carefree approach to life, and his blithe disregard for his wife's temper and shamanic powers. She might not turn him into a toad, because she wanted him, but she might not hesitate to reduce her guests to mushrooms in the snow. And what about my karma?

"So sorry, but I have to go to the bathroom now, all that cabbage for lunch!" and I rushed back to the house. I really did have to go. The turmoil he had just generated really agitated my intestines.

The other five guests, whose personalities had pretty much melted into car upholstery from the beginning, and I suffered through the last evening together. Mostly we munched popcorn in silence in front of the crackling fireplace. The next morning we donned hiking boots and trudged downhill in the snowy mud to the vehicles we had parked. Thankful to be dropped at the train depot at last, I expressed my gratitude to Emelda, whose eyes had turned dark gray with black currents running through them.

Thankful that my train reached its destination with me alive and intact, I took a streetcar to my home. Then I examined myself for thorns in the arteries or ravens flying overhead.

These days I limit my consumption of Portuguese wine at art receptions. And I do check references on people offering workshops and retreats. One really can't be too careful....

Fabulation or the Re-education of Undine

"FABULATION OR The Re-education of Undine" is the latest production to grace the stage of the Lorraine Hansberry Theatre. Opening night celebrated not only this wonderfully crafted and produced play, but also the LHT's triumph over adversity during its 30th season.

"Fabulation" gives us the hilarious and poignant tale of an ambitious woman in the time-honored American tradition, driven to be successful without regard for much else. All that glitters is all that matters. Margo Hall is superb as the glamorous exec who is dressed to kill and who cuts down all who get in her way. Undine Barnes Calles may have believed that all thoughts may be forgiven of her who has perfect candor, to quote Walt Whitman. "Generosity is expensive," Undine says. When prompting someone to get her surname right, she says it is pronounced like "callous."

Behind the authentic Gucci glasses and Louis Vuitton handbag, Undine is dancing on eggshells. Her accountant did not attend to business and neither did she. To be pregnant and broke, with the FBI suddenly investigating you for fraud, is not part of a career executive's game plan. And your society friends can't afford to know you anymore. There are many sins which are acceptable in that life style; being broke is not one of them.

Margo Hall clearly loves the character she plays, from Undine's stylish arrogance in Manhattan to the woeful moment when she drags herself back, all the way back, to her blue collar relatives in the Walt Whitman public housing projects of Brooklyn, where they remember her as "Sharona." How did you find us, they ask Undine sarcastically, since you told the press we died in a fire years ago?

There are many funny moments, cleverly staged and wonderfully acted, as Undine gets back in touch with her Sharona. A little encounter with smack; fabrication as our heroine scams her way through drug rehab; an obscenely accurate confrontation with the Social Services bureaucracy; a developing awareness that childhood friends have gone beyond blue collar status without selling their souls; and a belated understanding that pregnancy does not ignore you just because you ignore it.

Lynn Nottage wrote "Fabulation." She also wrote "Ruined," which won the Pulitzer Prize. Nottage has received a Guggenheim fellowship and a MacArthur genius grant.

Walt Whitman said I celebrate myself, and sing myself. He also said I exist as I am, that is enough. Does Undine finally discover the simple brilliance of this perspective on life? You'll have to see the play to find out.

JEANNE POWELL

Fela!

FELA! IS THE STORY of legendary Nigerian musician Fela Kuti, whose soulful Afrobeat rhythms ignited a generation all over the world. His life story of courage, passion and controversy is told through Kuti's captivating music along with the visionary choreography of Bill T. Jones. This is so much more than a musical and it keeps the audience rocking for 2-1/2 hours.

Fela Kuti (1938-1997) has been described by Gene Santoro in *The Nation* as a "mix of shaman, politician, ombudsman, activist and musical genius." Raised in Nigeria, musically educated in England (where he discovered American jazz and blues) and politically awakened in the United States (where he was exposed to the civil rights movement), Fela became to the Nigerian people what reggae genius Bob Marley was to the citizens of Jamaica.

Many of Kuti's concerts were held in his nightclub (The Shrine) in the city of Lagos, Nigeria, and this setting is reproduced onstage. Sahr Ngaujah is mesmerizing as Kuti, showcasing talents which made Kuti famous – accomplished musician, singer, dancer and polemicist.

Because of Kuti's high visibility and strong opposition to the Nigerian government, he was beaten, arrested and jailed numerous times. Fela's powerful songs ridiculed and condemned governmental corruption, police brutality, and exploitation of his country by multinational corporations.

To keep the audience informed, contemporary newspaper headlines and Fela's song lyrics are superimposed on small screens bordering the stage. Those who don't know the story, or don't care about the origins of this amazing music, may just rock along with the dancers and musicians. You don't need to know the story to dance in rhythm with Afrobeat.

Kuti's inspiration was his beloved Yoruba mother, Funmilayo, portrayed by Melanie Marshall. Fela never recovered from her death at the hands of government troops, who raided his Lagos compound (nightclub and living quarters) and burned it to the ground in 1977. Deep in grief at one point, he wishes to speak to Funmilayo and calls upon the god Shango, the orisha of fire, for permission to visit the spiritual afterworld. The staging for this sequence is stunning, and this high level of stagecraft is maintained throughout the play.

Bill T. Jones conceived, directed and choreographed this musical. Jones received a Tony award in 2009 for his choreography in Fela! Jones is the recipient of a MacArthur genius grant.

Wanjiru Kamuyu and Jill Marie Vallery are dance captains for this vibrant production. Jermaine Rowe is the assistant dance captain.

Producers for Fela! include actor Will Smith, actor Jada Pinkett Smith, and music mogul Jay-Z.

JEANNE POWELL

12 Years A Slave

British film director Steve McQueen has given us an unforgettable depiction of slavery in the antebellum south, one which will provide for most Americans their deepest education yet on why slavery in the New World was a form of genocide. McQueen creates his indelible images in "12 YEARS A SLAVE" through a combination of casting, photography and a careful reading of Northup's memoir of that terrible period in one man's life.

Solomon Northup was born a free man in New York state in 1808. He married Anne Hampton on Christmas Day 1829, and they had three children. In 1841 he was drugged, sold into slavery and transported to the Deep South where he struggled to survive for 12 desperate years before regaining his freedom. Northup's memoir was published in 1853.

Slavery was a crucial aspect in the development of the New World's prosperous economic system (1500s into 1800s). The plantation economies of North America and Latin America depended on slave labor. White men refused to do the work, so it was decided to enslave Native

Americans until they were exterminated, and then to kidnap Africans at gunpoint and transport them to the Americas in order to build wealth for the Europeans.

Solomon Northup's memoir speaks for itself, and McQueen realizes that. He allowed this searing record to unfold on the screen as it was written.

Most of us think we know what goes on in the city or town where we live, and we would be wrong. Recall the periodic media revelations of sweat shops, massage parlors and abuse in schools right in our midst, for example. Imagine the feeling of amazement experienced by Solomon Northup when he woke up half naked and chained in a dank basement cell, right in the heart of Washington D.C. How could such a thing happen in the heart of his nation's capital, he wondered. How can this be?

The actor who plays Northup has said "this man is slipping down the rabbit hole into another universe." Northup is told that from now on, his name is Platt. But he never forgets that he is Solomon Northup; for 12 years he clings to that name through all kinds of challenges and danger, until his memories and his determination are rewarded.

For actor Chiwetal Ejiofor, the challenge was to get inside Northup's state of mind and then show the complete and utter disbelief at his new status as a kidnap victim. He protests, only to be beaten into submission by the slave catchers. Another kidnap victim recognizes that Northup is a first-time enslaved, and warns him not to protest too much, or he will be killed. It is good advice. One brave enslaved man protests when he sees a white mariner about to rape a female kidnap victim, and he is killed on the spot.

From the leisurely life of a free family man in New York, Northup is transported into a hell he had never experienced. Dinner with new white friends, Brown (Scoot McNairy) and Hamilton (Taran Killam), in Washington D.C. results in his being drugged and transported to a dungeon. At night he is chained and forced to travel by wagon to a steamboat which takes him downriver, and so is sold eventually to a plantation owner in New Orleans.

The other enslaved survivors he meets on this twelve year journey, along with the various slave dealers and slave owners, comprise his new world. We witness what he experiences and see him struggle to respond in ways which allow him to survive.

Chiwetal Ejiofor's fine performance as Solomon Northup is matched by other depictions in the film. Michael Fassbinder is riveting as Edwin Epps, a plantation owner so immersed in his addiction to power that he does not see its corrosive impact on his marriage.

Sarah Paulson is chilling as his perfectly groomed wife seething with frustrated anger. She demands that her husband sell young Patsey (stunning performance by Lupita Nyong'o) to another plantation; Epps refuses and continues to rape Patsey when he chooses. Unable to stop Epps from going to Patsey's bed, Mistress Epps begins to physically attack her so as to make the helpless girl unattractive to Epps. Bewildered and desperate, at one point Patsey asks Northup to please kill her so she can escape her torment; he is afraid and so refuses.

The above dilemma is one of several moral crises which Northup must face as he struggles to determine where he can make a difference, and where he must stand aside and allow others to suffer so that he can survive.

An interesting cameo by Alfre Woodard as Mistress Shaw, the African American wife of a white plantation owner, reminds us that in Louisiana sometimes an enslaved mistress could rise above Patsey's desperate plight, as long as there was no white woman on the plantation.

Some have quibbled over a cameo by superstar Brad Pitt, one of the film's producers. He appears briefly as a Canadian traveling through the U.S. and its territories, working as a carpenter, which is how he meets Northup; and he is convincing in his role. The fact that he is recognizable as Brad Pitt hardly qualifies as a reason to keep him off camera.

Nigerian Chiwetel Ejiofor previously appeared in "Amistad" with Anthony Hopkins and Morgan Freeman, as well as "American Gangster" with Denzel Washington and Russell Crowe. Alfre Woodard starred in "Steel Magnolias" with Phylicia Rashad and Jill Scott; and she appeared in "Down in the Delta" with Wesley Snipes and Al Freeman Jr.

Filmed on five locations in Louisiana, this film surrounds Solomon Northup with the physical environment of the antebellum south – humid hot weather, the lush beauty of tropical vegetation, plantation crops demanding constant attention (sugar cane and cotton), challenges of felling trees and creating lumber, the sound of cicadas. The gorgeous cinematography is by Sean Bobbitt, who has worked with McQueen on previous films.

As more than one critic has implied, "12 YEARS A SLAVE" is about a holocaust, specifically the vastly underreported details of slavery as practiced in the United

States and its territories. Thanks to the efforts of director Steve McQueen and producer Brad Pitt, the harsh reality of antebellum slavery may finally receive recognition.

This is a film for the ages.

My Big Adventure

"COME UP TO POINT ARENA and read for me." OK, why not? Even though I have no idea where Point Arena is, I think it cannot be too hard to find. So I schedule this event in the distant future, and ask for a street address. "Well, we don't really use street addresses here – it's the red building with flowers in front. We only have one main road." OK. That's something they do in Carmel, right? Small town, people all know each other, streets have no names. Sure, no problem. Now, how do I get there? "GGT will take you to Santa Rosa. There may be some local bus after that. Just ask someone to drive you instead."

So I call Dude and ask him to drive me to Mendocino in April, and he says "yeah" because it's Mendocino, right? Two days before the event, Dude calls and says it's been a bad week: the car went up in flames, an old flame surfaced with spectacular woes, and his employer is imploding. So the Mendocino trip is no longer on his calendar.

Canceling a spoken word gig at the last minute is not good for a poet's reputation, so I call Petaluma folks and San Rafael folks and ask what they know about getting to Point Arena and whether they know anyone in Santa Rosa who would like to drive to this reading. No help there – people are tied up or don't know where Point Arena is, or both.

Recuperating from a spider bite and grading student essays, I'm getting worried. I visit my friend Kate and she looks up Mendocino transit info on Google while I play with her baby daughter. Transit options for Point Arena are not good.

Then I slap myself to pull out of the doldrums and decide this is going to be a great reading, even though I'm not sure where it is. Continuing to leave status reports on my host's cell phone, which I find out later she can't access in Point Arena, I move merrily along. Gathering strawberries, raisin bread, bottled chai latte and my favorite lipstick, I pack a small bag and head for GGT on the appointed day. The driver miraculously knows something about Mendocino transit because "someone asked me that question last week," he said. A sign from the Muse – this reading is going to happen!

At the driver's suggestion, I leave that particular GGT bus and board another one. The new driver says, "Yeah, I'm supposed to get to the depot at 4pm but sometimes I'm late so don't count on it because of traffic, and one time I was two hours behind schedule." Appropriately downcast, I sit on the new bus and wait out the ride. After the GG Bridge, we hit the freeway and hardly ever stop – a good sign. We reach Santa Rosa only five minutes late. I search frantically for the Mendocino connection, asking three GGT drivers, who all say they don't know anything about the local buses going to smaller communities, giving that info is not in their job description, etc. As a last resort, I go into "pre-crying" mode with the third driver, who hastily summons help on his walkie-talkie. As if by magic, someone in a midnight blue vest appears and walks me to the right waiting area. He even holds the bus while I go to the water closet.

What a grand bus ride – positively grand. About 20 passengers on a jitney bus, with everyone eating and drinking and laughing. We exchange business cards. Someone takes out a checkbook and writes a check to pay for my book, WORD DANCING. Hairpin turns with danger lurking at nearly every turn. Really big rocks far below in the wet sand, steep grassy cliffs, diamond blue ocean waves crashing on the shore below, bright sunlight dancing everywhere. Cattle, horses, sheep and wild deer dot the hillsides.

The sweet elder sitting in front of me is eating a ton of peanut butter cookies, and cookie aroma mixed with hairpin turns produces a little queasiness for me. I strap myself in – you betcha there are seat belts on this ride – and take a nap. Perhaps there is an uncertain look on my face because I hear the driver call out, "I have ginger candy for anyone whose stomach is doing flipflops."

With all that eating and drinking going on, some people cannot wait for the one scheduled rest stop. Whenever anyone calls out for water closet relief, the driver cheerily obliges, pulling into a state park or a gas station. Once we arrive in Point Arena, some people ask to be delivered to their door, rather than the bus stop. And the driver is happy to do so. I request the red building with flowers in front, and I'm delivered to that door, only 30 minutes late.

But I'm right on time for the reading. An attentive audience of locals, who really come for the poetry. They listen. It is an awe-inspiring experience. They really listen. And they buy books.

My host and friend puts me up for the night. We eat home-canned preserves and organic bread. After she assures me there are no bears, I go to sleep in a little house in the big woods, and have the most wonderfully relaxed sleep. I wasn't concerned about wolves or antelope or red-tailed hawks, little foxes or mountain lions – just bears.

And the next morning, I get to take the delightful jitney bus again, with some of the same riders. It doesn't get any better than this.

The Business of Bowing

PROTOCOL IS POLITICAL.

KENNEDY: Once upon a time Jacqueline Kennedy wondered whether she should curtsy to the queen when she and her husband were planning to visit England. After all, she had curtsied when she and her sister Lee visited the UK years earlier. Wisely, she consulted her husband's chief of protocol, and he said: "the wife of a chief of state does not curtsy." Problem solved before it became a problem. The Kennedys dined with the royal couple in private during their visit to England.

REAGAN: Nancy Reagan said out loud that she "wasn't going to curtsy to anyone" when she and her husband visited the UK. Unfortunately, her remark was repeated, and she was the object of derision before she ever set foot in the palace. It is good to consult the chief of protocol, Nancy found out. She and her husband dined with the queen and hundreds of others, at one of those state dinners the queen hosts when she really doesn't like her guests and is being nice at the request of the PM.

THATCHER: The other night on a "Frontline" documentary, I saw a vintage video clip of former PM

Margaret Thatcher being greeted at a foreign airport by dignitaries. She shook hands with all, except the last man presented to her. She took his hand, and gave a deep curtsy. Not likely to be off her game when it comes to protocol, Margaret must have been meeting a prince of the blood or a king. But wasn't she a chief of state back then? If so, why did she curtsy? Possibly because the queen is the chief of state in England, even though political power is exercised by the PM? OK, that works for me.

OBAMA: We all know that first lady Michelle put her arm around the queen when America's first couple visited the UK recently, and we've all heard that one doesn't touch the queen. Apparently the queen was not bothered. After all, the Obamas dined in private at the palace with Elizabeth and Philip.

Now the juicy part – did President Obama really bow to the Saudi king? We could not hear the dialogue in the video clip, but the king was smiling broadly during this public introduction. Was there a shared joke? Was Obama deliberately fanning the fears of American reactionaries, who still fear that he is a secret Muslim?

For some reason, I'm enjoying this entire subject immensely. So little is funny these days in the international news.

The Invisible War

A STUNNING DOCUMENTARY about a national tragedy.

In November 2011, California Congresswoman Jackie Speier introduced a bill in the House of Representatives to reform the way rape crimes are treated in the U.S. military.

This overdue legislation was introduced in response to an epidemic of rape and sexual assault of military women, committed by men in the military, which the Pentagon has known about for years – sexual assault at the prestigious military academies, at American bases foreign and domestic, and in war zones such as Iraq and Afghanistan – where a military female is more likely to be raped by her colleagues than killed by enemy soldiers.

In her press release Speier stated, "For too long the military's response to rape victims has been: 'take an aspirin and go to bed.' We owe our brave women and men in the military a justice system that protects them, not punishes them, when they become victims of sexual assaults and rape committed by other service members."

Representative Jackie Speier added, "Despite 25 years

of Pentagon studies, task force recommendations and congressional hearings, sexual assaults and rape in the military continue unabated. In 2010 the Department of Defense conducted a survey of active duty members which revealed that only a small percentage of the more than 19,000 incidents of rapes and sexual assaults involving service members was actually reported. For the record, an estimated 13.5 percent of sexual assaults and rapes saw the light day—and only 8 percent of those reports resulted in prosecution—in the end 465 service members were either administratively discharged or punished through the court-martial process —that's about 2.5 percent of the total suspected acts of sexual assaults and rape...."

THE INVISIBLE WAR is an award-winning documentary which exposes official propaganda and points out that the Pentagon seems to be supporting a culture of rape and oppression despite lip service to the contrary with phrases such as "zero tolerance" and "everything in our power" [is being done].

This remarkable and poignant film contains interviews with more than a dozen military women (and a few men) whose lives were devastated as a result of sexual assault in the Coast Guard, Marines, Army, Air Force and Navy. The perpetrators were their colleagues, comrades, brothers in arms, and frequently their commanding officers. The betrayal is made worse by the career devotion of these patriotic enlistees and their trust in the system.

As though this reality of sexual assault and rape were not bad enough, behavioral experts in the documentary testify to the fact that many of the offenders are likely to be serial rapists, both in the military and later in civilian retirement, with as many as 300 victims overall per rapist – such is the nature of the protection they receive from the Pentagon's insistence on preserving absolute authority in the chain of command.

In 2011 military veteran Susan Burke, Esq. brought a lawsuit on behalf of several of these rape survivors, alleging violation of Due Process clause, Equal Protection clause and First Amendment rights, only to have a federal court dismiss the suit with the remark, "rape is an occupational hazard of military service," according to THE INVISIBLE WAR.

Congresswoman Speier's proposed legislation would remove the oversight and investigation of military rape from the traditional chain of command, and would allow rape survivors to transfer to other units. Speier has over 100 co-sponsors for this bill, and the support on Capitol Hill is bi-partisan.

The stories of these rape survivors are chilling, as they speak in subdued voices of the calculating and often violent nature of the attacks. Several survivors suffered permanent physical damage, in addition to the obvious emotional trauma. Yet the Pentagon continues to allow this conduct in an all-volunteer military where the nation depends on the skills and dedication of female volunteers as much as males.

Kori's story is primary in THE INVISIBLE WAR. Kori is a Coast Guard seaman who suffered permanent nerve damage as a result of violent rape by her supervisor. Despite a 70% disability rating, the Veterans Administration refuses to pay for the surgery she needs. Her husband left the Coast Guard because of his wife's experience. The strain on their marriage is evident, with tears in the husband's eyes as he says he will never allow their daughter to join the military.

In another powerful moment, an active duty marine breaks down as he speaks of the ever-present fear that his accomplished wife will commit suicide because of the rapes she suffered at a prestigious Marine base in Washington D.C. The military men who raped her said they will kill her if she tries to prosecute.

This straight-forward documentary may be powerful enough to change the Pentagon mindset and bring about reform that is overdue. Congresswoman Jackie Speier spoke in San Francisco recently when the film opened at the Metreon, urging community support around this issue. Present were several rape survivors, some of whom are featured in THE INVISIBLE WAR.

The film is directed by Kirby Dick. Music is by Mary J. Blige, with Gary Calamar as music supervisor. Influential executive producers include Jennifer Siebel Newsom, director and producer of "Miss Representation," an acclaimed documentary which explores the harm resulting from the media's distorted images of women.

Beyond the urgent need to enact legislation introduced by Jackie Speier in the House of Representatives, perhaps there is an equally strong need to look closely at the American culture which glamorizes sexual assault in television series, films and video games. Dressing women in clothing favored by prostitutes – which fashion designers admitted doing when they ran out of ideas – sends another negative message about young women in our society.

And we may wish to ask for an evaluation of how recruits are brought up to speed by drill sergeants and training instructors in all branches of the military. Is it necessary to refer to new male recruits as "ladies, girls, wimps, pussies and c*nts" when instructors want to jeer at their lack of physical skill? What are the values and backgrounds of these noncoms placed in charge of training vulnerable recruits?

Especially compelling in THE INVISIBLE WAR are the moments when rape survivors travel to Capitol Hill and tell their experiences to several of Representative Speier's female colleagues. When one Congresswoman says, "I know what you are going through," we are reminded how much the crime of rape has infected our society on every level.

It is worth remembering that in 1777 sixteen-year-old Sybil Ludington rode on horseback all night in the rain, going from farm to farm to warn her father's troops that the British were coming and to return to base immediately. Despite the obvious multiple dangers, this "daughter of the regiment" accepted the emergency assignment and served well. Ludington was celebrated for her accomplishment – celebrated – and not resented because she had the ability and courage to do her job.

If you wish to help stop the epidemic of rape in today's military and make a genuine difference, instead of sitting back and pretending you cannot influence anything, then take the following action:

[1] go to http://speier.house.gov/ to learn more.

[2] visit Rep. Speier on Facebook and Twitter if you prefer social sites.

[3] go to http://protectourdefenders.com and get involved.

[4] see THE INVISIBLE WAR; take friends/family/neighbors/colleagues.

Rape may be an occupational hazard of war, but it is not and must not be an occupational hazard of serving among colleagues in our own military.

Connections

EARLY ON A FOGGY Sunday morning and I am running late. Shaking off the natural urge to slow-stretch and go back to sleep, I gather what seems useful and pour everything into whatever oversized purse I'm using that day.

Last Sunday of the month and we poetry lovers are meeting at Deborah's lovely home in Walnut Creek. I tumble down the hill to BART and settle into my seat as soon as I determine whether I'm on the right train or whether I have to change at MacArthur.

After putting on jewelry and running fingers through my hair, I take a short nap. At some point I telephone Alex and say that BART is running late. Early in the morning on a Sunday, and I have told a lie. BART is on time; I am the one who is running late.

Alex is waiting at BART and gives me a ride in his dusty pickup; he's been pulling weeds and taming the vegetation growing wild in his yard. We find parking easily in Deborah's driveway and enter into the serene coolness of her living room. Today our salon will focus on the war poets, veterans of the First World War such as

Rupert Brooke, Wilfred Owen, Siegfried Sassoon, Guillaume Apollinaire.

In Deborah's sunny kitchen are freshly brewed coffee and a variety of teas, with hot water on the stove. Some guests bring desserts they baked and others supply fruit from farmers markets. Alex feeds us organic corn chips and potato chips, for those who love salty snacks. We begin.

But I've a rendezvous with Death
At midnight in some flaming town,
When Spring trips north again this year,
And I to my pledged word am true,
I shall not fail that rendezvous.
— **Alan Seeger,** a favorite poem of President JFK.

Your battle-wounds are scars upon my heart,
Received when in that grand and tragic "show"
You played your part two years ago,
And silver in the summer morning sun
I see the symbol of your courage glow —
That Cross you won two years ago …
— **Vera Brittain,** British nurse in WW I; she lost her lover, her brother and a third friend.

None saw their spirits' shadow shake the grass,
Or stood aside for the half used life to pass
Out of those doomed nostrils and doomed mouth,
When the swift iron burning bee
Drained the wild honey of their youth….
— **Isaac Rosenberg,** British portrait artist and poet; died 1918.

As we read and discuss, I notice fruit trees partially visible from the living room window. Before we leave that day, Deborah and her husband take us outside to gather persimmons and tangerines.

A day or so later, I take some persimmons and tangerines to an East Bay location where a Huna priestess is celebrating Hawaiian goddess Poli'ahu. Although she is the goddess of snow and ice and cold, Poli'ahu is revered because her melting snow provides fresh water, contributing to the health and well-being of the Hawaiian people. A fitting winter solstice celebration, and tropical fruit is welcomed.

The next evening I find myself on a Jesuit university campus, snacking on tangerine segments as I walk across the busy street. For some reason I pause and look back. A man parks his compact car across the street and gets out; he takes a prayer rug from the back seat and slowly looks around. In front of him the gently sloping lawn is empty this time of day. He begins to spread the prayer rug on the side of the hill; I smile and turn away as I finish my tangerine.

A hawk, one or two of which are campus residents, sails on air currents high above with wings spread wide. I remember that the hawk is a bird sacred to Poli'ahu. And I am most content, pleased with, and grateful for the compassion of this week.

JEANNE POWELL

Elysium

In the year 2159 there are two classes of people associated with the planet Earth: the vast majority of humans exist on an overpopulated and burned-out planet, and the very wealthy live on a beautiful space station called Elysium.

Matt Damon as Max represents the people of a ravaged Earth, and Jodie Foster as Secretary of Defense Delacorte defends the privileged population of space station Elysium. In this future world, computers control just about everything. These computers contain the software of your dreams, or your nightmares.

Neill Blomkamp wrote and directed this futuristic action drama. He also wrote and directed "District 9," and did the visual effects for "Stargate SG-1" and "Smallville," both for television.

The director has been quoted as saying, *"This isn't science fiction. This is today. This is now."*

Blomkamp employs vivid imagery so the viewer will see the connection between today's mindless destruction of the environment for short-term profit, and the decline in quality of life for the vast majority of Earth's inhabitants.

Max is born and raised on Earth but his hopes and dreams are connected to Elysium, which shines like a star in the night sky for a grubby youth raised in the slums of Los Angeles. At this time all of Los Angeles is a slum. He and his childhood friend, well played by Alice Braga, dream of a better life before circumstances separate them on Earth. Their brief reunion as young adults is tender and bittersweet.

The character of Max is the essential oppressed working man in 2159, lucky to have a job in this utterly defeated society. Suddenly he is placed in an impossible position due to an accident, and then what had been his long-term, long-shot pipe dream becomes a dire necessity. He must reach Elysium and he must do it in five days.

How Max achieves this goal takes the viewer through a richly detailed underworld which exists in every broken society – filled with brutally ironic humor, grimy resilience, wacko moments and occasional tenderness as the human spirit struggles to survive.

Secretary of Defense Delacorte's responsibility is protecting the outer-space suburb of Elysium from surprise visits by gritty Earth dwellers who have the expertise to repair abandoned space taxis and the desperation to try and get beyond Elysium's fearsome weaponry. She looks fabulous in Armani power suits and a million dollar haircut, and is ruthless in defending Elysium.

Max and Delacorte fight a war of strategy which turns into a mutual struggle for survival, rather than just another incursion into Elysium's air space.

What is startling here is that Max the factory worker and Delacorte the secretary of defense never meet, even though their actions and reactions have a profound impact on Elysium and on Earth.

Matt Damon's Max is a fully formed character from the boy who asks the nuns why he can't live on Elysium, to the convict who struggles to remain in the good graces of his automated parole officer, to the factory worker driven to risk everything to reach this fabled and fabulous place just out of his reach.

Jodie Foster would be able to do wonders with this delicious character, a secretary of defense in Armani suits who speaks French at endless receptions on Elysium, if only her part had been written with imagination and a focused intention. Instead what we have is a calculating war executive with no backstory and no real motivation. Her conflict with the president of Elysium lacks fire, seems artificial. It's simply difficult to believe she would not have employed more sophisticated responses to those pesky renegade space taxis entering unauthorized air space. And she acts alone without a trusted "number two" to cover her back.

Listen up, though – viewers who love gadgets and technology, who love space ships and weapons, advanced software and sophisticated robots will really enjoy this film. If you can get to it, there is a machine which will repair your mashed and mutilated body parts, if you can get there before you bleed out. And if you wish to know what it's like to receive bionic surgery without anesthetic or any of the other safeguards associated with cutting into your body, this film is right up your alley. A little bloody here and there, but the viewer receives a fascinating glimpse into the world of exoskeletons.

Foster's many fine films include The Brave One, Panic Room, Little Man Tate and The Accused. She first came to notice as a child performer in The Little Girl Who Lives Down the Lane and in Taxi Driver.

Damon's excellent performances include films such as Good Will Hunting, The Departed, the Bourne series and The Talented Mr. Ripley. He also narrated the internationally acclaimed documentary, INSIDE JOB, an award-winning film which explains the origins of the corporate greed which led to the recent destruction of national economies all over the world.

JEANNE POWELL

Vantage Point

"VANTAGE POINT" is a political thriller from Columbia Pictures, directed by Pete Travis, and it does hold your attention on more than one level.

Leaders of several countries gather in Salamanca, Spain, for a conference on "terrorism." The city's central square holds up to 20,000 people and it is crowded as president Ashton of the United States (William Hurt of "Eyewitness" fame) stands up to speak. Suddenly he is gunned down and officials run for cover. Secret Service agents Thomas Barnes (Dennis Quaid of "Far From Heaven") and Kent Taylor (Matthew Fox of "Emperor") help remove the president and search for suspects. A Spanish police officer hurtles toward the mayor of Salamanca, whose safety is his responsibility. A mystery woman tosses a satchel under the grandstand and disappears into the mass of citizens fleeing in panic. Sequestered in a nearby hotel suite, a presidential advisor promotes his own agenda. And American tourist Howard Lewis (Forest Whitaker of "Phone Booth" and "The Last King of Scotland") accidentally videotapes much more than he realizes.

One vantage point belongs to network news director Rex Brooks (Sigourney Weaver of "Alien" and "Year of Living Dangerously") as she orchestrates multiple cameras to reflect her own sense of political theater. But then the assassination attempt, bomb explosions and a mortally wounded journalist (Zoe Saldana of "Avatar") have an impact on her agenda.

With each rewind, the perspective changes and the mystery deepens. The viewer is reminded of "Roshomon," Akira Kurosawa's 1951 classic with four distinct versions of a crime. And "The Seige," Edward Zwick's stunning 1998 film which focuses on a secret American abduction of a suspected insurgent leader and the violent consequences which follow.

"Vantage Point" moves at breakneck speed, with a chase scene more exciting than Steve McQueen's in "Bullitt" or Robert DeNiro's in "Ronin." And the complexity of motives on all sides is portrayed absorbingly.

The viewer may wish to recall General Wesley Clark's remarks regarding Paul Wolfowitz in 1991 and also the infamous "Seven Countries Memo" which became known to Clark in 2001. Then ask yourself, who actually is the enemy? What defines a terrorist? What do we know? What do we really know? Who's zooming whom?

JEANNE POWELL

The Other Boleyn Girl

IN ANTICIPATION OF revisiting one of my favorite historical periods, I waited in line to see "The Other Boleyn Girl," directed by Justin Chadwick. New perspective, what's not to like, I thought. I even invited one of my friends to join me at the Metreon cinema south of Market Street. After the preview, Barry and I drowned our cinematic sorrows around the corner at Jillian's restaurant, and that was expensive grieving.

Look, there is a reason poor little Mary is known as the other Boleyn girl, to the extent she is known at all. She simply did not have an impact on history. Despite the best efforts of Scarlett Johansson as Mary Boleyn and Eric Bana as King Henry VIII, this "rice crispy" version of little Mary's soap-opera life does not signify.

King Henry VIII ruled England from 1509 to 1547. He married six times; he divorced two of his wives and executed another two. One died in childbirth and the last one managed to outlive him. He was a ruthless lecher, among other things, but we're still fascinated by him and his times. Mary Boleyn, "the other Boleyn girl," gave in to the predatory king too soon, and she became a footnote in Tudor history. Anne held out for a crown and became the mother of Elizabeth, one of England's great queens. Henry had his wife Anne killed when their daughter was a toddler.

So much rich history, which has been filmed many times, both for the big screen and for television's Masterpiece Theatre over the years. At best this new film is about beautiful costumes and well-groomed horses galloping along tree-lined paths from one medieval house to another. At worst it's filled with trivial dialogue and misleading history.

Natalie Portman really is convincing as Anne Boleyn, the famous "Anne of a Thousand Days," brought to life so beautifully by Genevieve Bujold in the 1969 Charles Jarrot film. However, Portman's best efforts as Anne are sabotaged by second-rate writing. In the earlier Bujold film, a play by Maxwell Anderson was adapted for the screen. In "The Other Boleyn Girl," a novel by Philippa Gregory is the inspiration. Both Gregory and the screenwriter who adapted her work have "credentials," but no amount of acting, editing or explaining could salvage this unfortunate script.

The Tudor period with its cold-blooded kings and unhappy queens remains popular, filled as it is with power struggles, assassinations, religious purges, and graphic exploitation of young female nobility. Kingdoms and empires rose and fell on the basis of whose wife could produce a healthy heir. That's why Anne Boleyn's story continues to fascinate, as does that of her murderous husband, Henry VIII, and her brilliant daughter, the first Queen Elizabeth. Mary Boleyn's story, on the other hand, does not arouse one's interest at all.

See this film for the horses, rich costumes, countryside views, well-preserved medieval houses, and good performances by Scarlett Johansson and Natalie Portman. Ignore the script.

Mad Money

IN BRINGING "Mad Money" to the screen, director Callie Khouri works with a script based on a true story. Knowing that this landmark heist happened in England, and that it was pulled off by three women in working-class jobs, armed only with their wits, is a delight to savor.

Diane Keaton is a suburban matron accustomed to a very good life until her husband, Ted Danson, loses his prestigious position and remains unemployed as the months go by. She is amazed to discover they are some $260,000 in debt and their mansion is about to go on the market. When her personal check to pay the housekeeper bounces, Keaton tries to pay the exasperated woman with a silver-plated water pitcher.

Queen Latifah and Katie Holmes already are employed as janitors at the Federal Reserve Bank when socialite Keaton is hired as their co-worker, the only job with health insurance she could find.

Latifah is a dedicated single mom raising two young sons in the best job available. This turn is 180 degrees from Latifah's last film venture as a bandit, "Set It Off," directed by Gary Gray (1996). In the earlier movie, Latifah starts robbing banks with two other underpaid housekeepers, but their provocative adventure ends in a bloody shootout with police.

Holmes plays a diabetic with daffy ways, who loves to listen to rock and roll throughout her shift at the Federal Reserve Bank. Earbuds firmly in place, she dances through the parking lot on her way to work. Holmes is carefree in this film, playing a part quite different from her traumatized character in Joel Schumacher's "Phone Booth" (2002).

Security is everywhere at the bank, and everything is done by the book. The lives of Keaton, Latifah and Holmes are not nearly so secure. Flexibility and creativity govern their existence as they reinvent their lives in a time of great financial inequity. Their interactions with each other, their employer and the men in their lives are authentic and funny.

One of the highlights in Keaton's comedic moments on film will be the scene where the bank manager sweats under the stony gaze of federal cops and attorneys, unwilling to admit the possibility that anything actually happened on his watch. He stares through a glass partition at an elegantly dressed Keaton, who uses her animated body language to convey, "you can't touch this!"

Lots of twists and turns in this thoroughly enjoyable caper film. "Mad Money" is intriguing in its focus on nonviolent felonies requiring creativity, and the possible inevitability of such crimes during times of significant social injustice. Plenty of laughter and surprises here, especially for those who appreciate life's ironies. And a classic rock and roll soundtrack!

The Iron Lady

BRITISH PRIME MINISTER Margaret Thatcher portrayed by Meryl Streep, yes – who else? Another bravura performance by one of the four greatest actresses in the western world. Compelling performances also are delivered by Jim Broadbent as Thatcher's husband Denis and Alexandra Roach as young Margaret.

Directed by Phyllida Lloyd, a major figure in British theater and film, "The Iron Lady" is an ambitious portrait of Britain's most controversial PM and the only PM to be elected to three consecutive terms.

Margaret Thatcher was elected to the House of Commons in 1959 and became prime minister of the UK in 1979. Although she resigned as PM in 1990 to avoid a defeat within her own party, Thatcher continued to serve in the House of Commons for another two years. The queen bestowed a title on her in 1992, and then appointed Baroness Thatcher to the House of Lords.

Thatcher was the only child of a grocer. She attended Oxford University and trained as a chemist. Later she became an attorney (barrister), married a businessman, gave birth to fraternal twins and changed the course of British history, pretty much in that order. Because of her opposition to Marxism and the USSR, the former Soviet Union branded her "the iron lady."

Someone once said Meryl Streep could recite the telephone directory and produce Oscar material. Screenwriter Abi Morgan has provided a much better script than that, but with a soft focus on Thatcher's hard core political views and actions. The emphasis is on Thatcher in retirement and intellectual decline, living through her memories after suffering a series of small strokes. While Streep is able to handle this phase of Thatcher's life extremely well, the viewer is left wondering how much more exciting it would have been to see Thatcher in a chronological portrait of her tempestuous political career.

Margaret Thatcher acted upon strongly held political views. She ended the program of free school milk for children over the age of seven, and increased the cost of school meals. In 1978 she made a speech where she claimed that people feared being "swamped" by immigrants. As prime minister she was determined to break the power of trade unions. Spending cuts led to a wave of strikes. The number of people unemployed doubled between 1979 and 1980. In 1984 coal miners struck for 12 months without success, due to the PM's iron will. She was indifferent to the continuation of the Commonwealth of Nations and indifferent to apartheid in South Africa. She also opposed any closer integration with Europe. And she imposed a poll tax on the people of the UK.

Director Phyllida Lloyd skillfully blends news video with realistic recreations. The PM and her husband narrowly escape death when their hotel is bombed by terrorists from the IRA. Before she becomes PM, one of Thatcher's advisors is killed by an IRA car bomb.

"The Iron Lady" offers a few tantalizing moments of Question Time in the House of Commons, where each week the prime minister must defend her actions or inactions before an eloquent and boisterous opposition. Lloyd and screenwriter Morgan enlisted all the right people to create a believable House of Commons, since they were not allowed to film in Parliament itself, and it would have been wonderful to have more of the PM's crises handled in this forum – highly entertaining as well as educational to the audience – but, no, this was not done. The 1982 Falklands naval war between England and Argentina was a complex business, both diplomatically and militarily. England lost three destroyers, two frigates and nearly 300 sailors; Argentina suffered even greater loss of life. That ill-advised war tested Thatcher but turned out to be a victory for the prime minister; yet the subject is reduced to a few short scenes in this film.

One glaring omission is any mention of the royals. Thatcher is said to have had more than one philosophical difference with the queen over the future of the Commonwealth of Nations, for example. Royal criticisms were leaked, since the queen may not oppose a prime minister openly. No mention of that here. When England went to war over the Falklands, the queen and Thatcher were seen in photo ops walking side by side to demonstrate solidarity; no glimpse of that in the film either.

Journalist Carol Thatcher has written about her mother; director Phyllida Lloyd utilizes that material to give us a portrait of a legend in winter. The PM's son,

Mark Thatcher, is absent from this film. Yet the only time Margaret Thatcher looked vulnerable was when her son went missing for several days during an international grand prix competition (Paris to Dakar).

Denis Thatcher is brought to life vividly by Jim Broadbent. Margaret Roberts married him in 1951; he died in 2003. By all accounts it was a very good match and he was proud of her. Too often, though, director Phyllida Lloyd employs imaginary conversations with the dead husband as a lens through which to view Margaret Thatcher in the present day.

Meryl Streep can do no wrong: The Devil Wears Prada (2006); The Manchurian Candidate (2004); The Bridges of Madison County (1995); Ironweed (1987); Out of Africa (1985); Plenty (1985) – my personal favorite; Silkwood (1983) – also my personal favorite; The French Lieutenant's Woman (1981).

See this film for the performances of Streep, Broadbent and Roach. For the actual history, visit a library or a bookseller.

Those Women In Veils

YOU KNOW THOSE WOMEN in veils, who are the subject of patronizing soundbites on American newscasts? Those women in veils who frequently appear as exotic subjects in lurid emails circulated by American liberals, who think of them as domestic drones paperclipped to a kitchen cabinet between photo ops?

Yeah. Those women. The ones we don't know because we haven't taken the time to read more about them, or to observe as they walk through our neighborhood every week. What's that, you say? They don't live in your neck of the woods? Well, whose fault is that?

They do live and/or work in my neighborhood. Various families from Yemen, Jordan, Afghanistan, Iraq, and other countries in Asia Minor can be found in my community – not just men going to and from the mosque, but women as well. Many of the women are wives and mothers, and they move about quite comfortably in their garments of choice – hijab, khimar, chador, niqab and burqa.

My impressions present very differently from the negative images American corporate media choose to throw at us.

There is the Irish-American who converted to Islam when she married a merchant from the Near East. They live in the suburbs, and she works on her master's degree at a local college. I believe she wears a khimar. And the African-American who converted when she married a Black Muslim. After passing the state bar exam, she now is practicing law. She wears an hijab.

The women who gather their children from an elementary school and walk home with them. These mothers walk in groups and are dressed in niqab or burqa, depending on the family's culture. Other women walking in twos or threes, sometimes with children, are dressed in chador. It's much easier to see their faces and to gauge reactions when I nod and smile.

Another wife and mother presides over a family grocery with regal dignity. Months after 9-11, I asked how she had fared. She and her husband put boards over the store windows after one was broken, and her two sons drove all night from college to get home and protect her in case the store was attacked again. While she chats easily with all customers in two languages, she declines the invitations of non-Muslim women to join them for tea at a local cafe near the mosque. She wears an hijab.

An elegant woman in a niqab shops in the neighborhood. With bracelets at her wrists and wearing modest high heels, she reveals more than is usual for someone wearing that garment. In the retail shops, she speaks only to the clerk behind the counter and pays in cash. We make eye contact sometimes. I watched her leaving a shop one day; she walked quickly and purposefully. Perhaps a car and driver were waiting around the corner?

I used to purchase snacks at a deli on Russian Hill; the owner was an immigrant with the look of a dynamic Old World prophet, pleasantly greeting all customers. One day I found him in front of the counter, quiet and holding a beautiful baby boy in his arms. Behind the display case, working in the food preparation area, was someone I knew immediately was his wife. Petite and graceful, fully covered, she wore a niqab. Only her hands and expressive eyes were visible. Her English was clear with the hint of an accent. Curious about me, as I was about her, she spoke first. Her world was her family, and she clearly was a presence in that family.

Recently newspaper photos featured a refugee camp in northern Yemen where beleaguered families lived in tents while military men disputed the surrounding territory. Women were seen carrying firewood gathered in the nearby desert; they wore straw hats on top of their niqab as they walked toward the tents where they now lived.

In terms of the Mujahideen and the Taliban, each of whom came to power at different times in Afghanistan – and who may have harmed any number of women in the name of God – it is important that we recall the heavy-handed American influence which led to the downfall of a moderate government in that country, and ushered in an era of ruthless insurgents and fundamentalists.

A few fatuous male functionaries in Egypt have challenged the right of Muslim students to remain covered while they live on campus at the University of Cairo, according to reports on PBS news programs and Agence France Presse. Last month women reported to the University and were locked out. They stood there in niqab, stunned and indignant, as they were interviewed by western press. Where were they going to live? Why weren't they warned in advance? And why were University officials violating the law, since a recent Supreme Court decision in Egypt affirmed the right of women to be veiled? PBS stations quoted an Egyptian bureaucrat as saying that one of the women "...is fat and ugly anyway, so she doesn't need to wear a veil." Well, all right then – and there we have it!

In this country women wear whatever the retail shops are selling, and frequently the designers of these clothes appear to have serious issues with women. Our faces are covered only with sunglasses. We walk about half naked, feeling liberated, right? And we all know how safe women are in this country. Let's see now, women and children are raped or sexually assaulted every hour of every day in the United States, or did we somehow overlook that reality? The advertising industry and its corporate clients in our free-market economy routinely exploit women's half-naked bodies in order to market every product and service imaginable. And video games – to which our teens are addicted – grow more violent with each new game. Oh, and the music, from which some recording executives make a lot of money? Don't even get me started on American popular music and its vicious imagery of women!

As Americans, we sometimes get the basics all fouled up. For example, all Muslims are not Arabs. All Arabs are not Muslims. The Persians of Iran are not Arabs. The Sikhs of India are not Muslims. The sons of Abraham seem to have issues with women, period, whether these sons are Jews, Christians or Muslims. The doctrinal divisions within Islam (Sunni, Shiia) are not any more problematic than the divisions within Christianity (Coptic, Catholic, Orthodox, Protestant) or Judaism (Conservative, Orthodox, Reform).

Muslim women vary as greatly as Christians or Jews in what they wear and how they fare in a world still dominated by male power struggles. You would think we Americans would know that. They matter to their families. And many are a power within their families. Perhaps we could pay them the respect they deserve, and not ridicule their decision to remain covered?

JEANNE POWELL

When a Legend Visits

Last month I tore myself away from answering emails and walked across campus to a convocation at a parish church. This was not a religious event, but the announcement read more like a summons than an invitation to assemble, perhaps because of the identity of the keynote speaker. The altar was hidden by draped fabric in front of which was a large video screen, with chairs to the left and a podium to the right.

This was a secular affair celebrating academic achievement where a college dean quoted Deuteronomy from the Old Testament; then the keynote speaker stepped forward and spoke for 30 minutes in spellbinding detail about our duty as citizens of this beleaguered planet.

I sat in a comfortable wooden pew near the front, the better to see the keynote speaker, he who had never wanted to be a legend or anything like it. As the dean invoked the name of the speaker's father and his father's image filled the video screen, quiet tears flowed down my face and I marveled at these tears, after all this time. His father was a young senator whom CBS news anchor Walter Cronkite labeled "a lion in the streets," who would not rest even for a second and who went where other public figures were afraid to go – the copper mines of Chile, plague-ridden urban neighborhoods, hovels in Appalachia.

The face of his martyred father filled the video screen behind the podium and I worried about the welfare of the keynote speaker. Had he been warned that his father's image would be displayed so long and his name invoked so often? He did not look at the screen as the dean spoke, and I held my breath even as tears continued to well up and spill down my cheeks.

I did not know this son of a legend, had never met him, yet knew all about him, more than most. Never had I heard him speak. At first his voice was hoarse from so many public appearances that I had to lean forward to catch his words. As he gathered momentum, the keynote speaker found his voice and was not troubled by the evocative image held so long on the screen behind him. He had found his cause in this life and has helped to make it ours, both by the skill of his arguments and the passion of his commitment.

As the richly robed academics left the church, I spotted someone I knew and walked with her to the reception, across the street and upstairs in a room with a view. Soon the keynote speaker appeared, to be lauded by academic leaders and listened to respectfully by well-placed alumni. After the applause, photo flashbulbs and the handshakes, he took a cell phone call from his son before preparing to leave for the airport.

Then I saw my chance. Carefully I prepared my words. I felt as though I had been waiting a long time to say them, not only for myself but also on behalf of so many others, and I did not realize it until now. The keynote speaker and I shook hands, and then I said *"I remember, I remember, I remember everything, and I want to thank you and your family for all that you have given to this country."*

He enveloped me in a sudden bear hug; I was overwhelmed. I said "thank you" and quietly moved away, remembering that others were waiting.

During the rest of the reception I felt a great peace descend on me. It is never too late to say thank you, and always wise to recall that others may not have done so, or may not have realized the need.

A skilled litigator on behalf of the environment, the keynote speaker teaches at a law school.

The Company You Keep

Robert Redford is back with a film we have been awaiting since the last Weather Underground activist came in from the cold at the end of the Carter administration. I do not mean to imply they all came in – only the ones who were tired of living a double life (Cathy Wilkerson in 1980), or who were caught in the commission of a crime (Kathy Boudin in 1981).

This political thriller about activists from the "days of rage" period is directed by Redford with a screenplay by Lem Dobbs. Neil Gordon wrote the novel on which the film draws. The script also was influenced by the disastrous 1981 Brinks robbery in New York in which three members of law enforcement died; Cathy Boudin and David Gilbert were among those arrested. During their imprisonment, their child was adopted by radicals Bill Ayers and Bernadine Dohrn. Years later, Ayers went on to become a friend of Barack Hussein Obama in another state.

As an influential actor, director, film producer and advocate for the environment, Redford had his pick of actors to tell the story of the subterranean radicals in Gordon's novel, and he attracted a brilliant cast to this film.

Redford plays an attorney and widower who lives quietly with his young daughter (Jackie Evancho). Shia LaBeouf is an irritatingly aggressive journalist for a small-town newspaper, intent on getting a Pulitzer (so he can keep his job). These radicals, who suddenly are news again when Susan Sarandon surrenders, were active before he was born. He smells a story and chases it without regard for consequences. In an attempt to establish communication during a jailhouse interview, Sarandon asks, "Do you have children?" "No," LaBeouf says, "I barely have furniture."

Julie Christie is an unrepentant leftist and sailor, using her boat to run marijuana across the Canadian border under the eyes of the Coast Guard. After all, she can't be a threat because she's just an old woman, right? Sarandon is a homemaker and well-loved wife with a perfect suburban life, along with a secret she no longer wishes to keep. Chris Cooper is Redford's brother, reluctant to be involved in his crisis, but family is family.

And Terrence Howard is perfect as the ambitious FBI supervisor, determined to get on top of this aging revolutionaries business, to finally bring in … somebody, so the feds won't look so incompetent. He is relentless, and he has technology the FBI did not have back in the day, when the Weathermen spun off from Students for a Democratic Society (SDS), and later became the Weather Underground.

Sam Elliott, Stanley Tucci, Richard Jenkins, Stephen Root, Susan Hogan and Nick Nolte round out the cast of veteran activists who successfully live like your neighbors next door, who are the neighbors next door. They have kept each other's secrets for such a long time now, never getting in touch unless absolutely necessary. Some are willing to help Redford when he goes on the run; others rebuff him in fear for their own carefully crafted situations.

"The Company You Keep" is both a political thriller and a morality play. What do you know about your neighbor next door? How long can someone live a lie? Is any act justified if the cause is righteous enough? And what about the people who have to pay for your mistakes – the bank guard who died in the botched bank robbery, for example, in Neil Gordon's novel? So many secrets, and what does an arrogant young journalist know or care about secrets?

Redford shows us many tricks as a fugitive with multiple IDs and disposable cell phones, and as someone who knows how to blend in a crowd, but there is something odd about the way he is running. Where is he going, and why? The suspense caused by his mysterious journey and by the pit bull tendencies of the young journalist carries the film.

In addition to the grieving families who lost loved ones when political crimes went awry, there are the children of the radicals – the ones they raised and the ones they gave to others for safety reasons. Sarandon turns herself in because of her children. Redford has to put his young daughter in safe hands before going on the run. And there are others…

For a while now there has been a need to revisit this subject in American consciousness, and not simply whenever the FBI has an arrestee in tow. We have Marge Piercy's superb novel, VIDA, containing incredible detail about that period; Piercy was at University of Michigan with Tom Hayden, future California legislator. Hayden may or may not have been one of those involved in writing the first draft of the Port Huron Statement for SDS.

There is the excellent novel, *Downriver,* written by Peter Collier before his right-wing days. And there is a haunting memoir by a young FBI agent, one of the first to be sent deep undercover and who operated illegally in Canada. He never got into the inner circle of the Weather Underground, which by then was said to be run by women, but the experience affected him so deeply that he resigned and went to live in the mountains, not unlike some combat veterans from the American war in Vietnam.

In the wake of an unprecedented number of domestic assassinations in the 1960s, political and social activity took on a new intensity – the civil rights movement and resistance to the military draft, among others. This period also included the activism of revolutionary movements around the world as a direct result of rising expectations after World War II. The radicalization of thousands of youth from comfortable and even wealthy families on every continent should not have been such a surprise; but apparently it was. See also Cathy Wilkerson's *Flying Close to the Sun* and Susan Braudy's *Family Circle* (concerning Kathy Boudin) about the company they kept.

An excellent accomplishment by Robert Redford, on a subject which has needed a good film for a long time.

"Protest beyond the law is not a departure from democracy; it is absolutely essential to it."

– Historian Howard Zinn

City Scenes

[1]

Saturday evening late, I walked past a well-known tea emporium, and noticed a private party in full swing with live music and guests in costume. The owner was celebrating his birthday and commanded all guests to dress as their inner selves, or their favorite fantasies. Two uniformed schoolgirls sucking on candy pacifiers were exiting as I chatted with one of the musicians, who used to live two doors down from me. He left his former apartment when the owner converted the building to TICs (tenancies in common) and he couldn't afford to purchase his unit; the owner paid each tenant $5,000 to move. You could have gotten much more, I said. I know, he responded, but I didn't want the hassle. Gleefully he added that the units mostly haven't sold, so the miserly owner is none the richer. Business hasn't been good for the large condominium complex down the hill either, which opened with bright signage and lots of balloons about three months ago. Real estate agents only show the building by appointment now. Even window signs announcing reduced prices have been taken down. However, the streets are cleaner than they used to be, and the homeless have moved to less ambitious neighborhoods. Yuppie newcomers from Silicon Valley seem to crowd the sidewalks these days, wearing ear buds and running gear, startling anyone who is out for a quiet stroll. And on weekend nights the upscale bars along Polk Street attract hundreds of the drunken dears, who stagger from bar to bar to ATM and back to the bars in designer clothes, protected by black-and-whites. Reminds me of the time when police thought they worked only for the wealthy. I miss the artists, carpenters and students who used to live around here. Even with rent control, they can't hang on – jobs simply disappear or work hours are reduced, or roommates move out and return to family homes in the east or midwest. Frequent sidewalk sales in several neighborhoods, where you can pick up a Le Creuset skillet or silver ice bucket for a song. And so it goes....

[2]

Last week my Webmaster called; he was between recording sessions and wanted to go for a drink. We stopped at a wine bar on Russian Hill. Nice ambience, only two other customers, and live music at the far end of the bar. After a moment he dashed out to move his motorcycle when a car seemed ready to back into it. Rejoining me, he said he really liked the new poem about the opera "Salome." Web drank two beers, which had no impact on him. I consumed two glasses of zinfandel and became bubbly. It should be said that I never drink two glasses unless I'm in the company of good friends. Why can't women drink like men? he mused. In the Mission where he grew up working construction, he learned to drink peers under the table. He just couldn't get over Serious Me becoming bubbly. We're smaller and our metabolism is complex, I suggested. As we munched salami, cheese and crackers, a "cigarette girl" walked in – right out of a classic Hollywood film – dressed for work in a night club, with a large tray supported by a heavy silk cord around her bare shoulders. Mints, candy, nuts, electronic roses? she smiled. What a surprise and where did you come from? I asked, examining the electronic roses. Oh, along here they pay me to circulate from club to club and I saw you two in the window looking happy so I thought you might want to purchase something, she replied. Web gave her the fish eye, so I prompted him – c'mon she's working here and she's nice; there must be something on the tray you would like. Finally I selected the mints at $3, right after she spoke about how heavy the tray was. Web was still giving her the fish eye when she strolled out. Really, guys can be so strange. How much will they spend on six-packs of beer and closed-circuit sports events – they'll drop an entire paycheck on that stuff. He insisted on walking me to the door of my building. It's raining and you're wearing heels and it's dark, he said. It's not raining that hard, my heels are only two inches and I know this area like the back of my hand, I countered, taking his arm. Women, he said, shaking his head. Yeah, I know; we rule, except when we work in clubs carrying heavy trays....

[3]

Fourth Street, positively, on a fog-filled afternoon – busy thoroughfare with electric buses, blaring taxis, tourists and local shoppers. Walking past a small hotel guarded by a doorman in full regalia, I encountered her, a character lost from the pages of Jean Rhys. She had been elegant once, the way she held her slender body unbent by age or financial calamity, the belief stored in her dark eyes, now wild from the exigencies of life, that one day she would be restored to her former glory. Something about the Hotel Palomar stopped her in freeze frame, returning her to those early days when suitors offered diamonds and pearls and said she would be a star always. Here she had dined in quiet splendor, received admirers, held her engagement party before her beloved died in a glorious foreign war. She was riveted to that spot in front of the hotel, accompanied by a tattered suitcase, her well-cut dress barely soiled, her face weathered by the sun without the benefit of rose oil to refine. She wanted to enter the Palomar, made a movement toward the entrance, guarded so firmly by the young doorman, who was determined to impress his employer with his dedication and awareness. And he was aware that she did not belong in there. No words were spoken; most walkers continued on their way without noticing the impasse, but I could not escape this confrontation. Her small shoulders leaned toward the double doors sparkling in afternoon light, and the doorman's knees flexed in readiness to block any move she made. Ignoring him, the lost lady stared at the hotel doors and windows, peering to catch a glimpse of those she once knew on the other side. Walls dissolved and reformed in her memory. Move and countermove on the sidewalk. I thought I could hear her screaming in the silence, but the doorman was not affected by her distress. She did not belong here now, of that he was certain, and she would not win this struggle. I wrenched myself away and walked along Fourth Street, toward traces of sunlight, grateful to escape into the present....

[4]

Riding Muni is how we roll, uphill and down in buses and trolleys, cable cars and streetcars, daylight and nighttime. Experience the vicissitudes of life on the 31 Balboa from Market to Eddy to Turk and finally Balboa, all the way to the ocean. I surely did, just the other day, riding to school first week of the month. Standing room only, windows won't open, assorted live animals loose in the aisles and lots of people happy to have cashed their checks – payroll, retirement, disability, unemployment compensation. Singing, laughing, yelling galore. Poetic wildness in the air and a full moon still visible through morning clouds. And exactly what is that they are smoking in the back of the bus? Feeling wobbly even before I inhaled, knee ligament mending slowly, I look around and ask for a seat, gesturing discreetly to my knee. A twenty-something looks up and enunciates perfectly the words, "I don't speak English!" Fearing the proliferation of all sorts of negative vibrations, I pull out my ancient cell phone and call a spiritual friend, who's cooking quinoa in her Sunset kitchen. Turning off the stove burner, she sits down right away and starts to chant Quan Yin verses just for me. *Bodhisattva/ infinite mercy/ divine compassion/ give me patience/ prevent me from killing her/ the one who uses perfect English/ to advise me that she speaks no English/ keep me free of hostile urges/ bless me Mother for I am sinning/* thoughts are running through my curly head until Allison's soulful chanting slows my heartbeat to a restful pace. And just then, some sweet soul says, "Would you like a seat?"

ABOUT THE AUTHOR

Jeanne Powell has earned degrees from WSU in Detroit and USF in San Francisco. She writes prose poems, flash fiction and short stage plays. Her previous books are MY OWN SILENCE and WORD DANCING, both published in second editions by Taurean Horn Press. For ten years Jeanne hosted an acclaimed spoken word series, "Celebration of the Word." She is the inspiration behind Meridien PressWorks™ which has published 20 authors since 1996. She has been an instructor in the CS, OLLI and UB programs in California.

jeanne-powell.com

starkinsider.com/author/jeannep

www.ingramcontent.com/pod-product-compliance
Lightning Source LLC
Chambersburg PA
CBHW020534120726
47904CB00003B/1067

* 9 7 8 1 5 8 7 9 0 2 6 6 6 *